Super Simple DIY SURVIVAL

DESIGN SURVIVAL CLOTHING YOUR WAY!

Crafting Weatherproof Wearables

ELSIE OLSON

CONSULTING EDITOR, DIANE CRAIG,
M.A./READING SPECIALIST

Super Sandcastle

An Imprint of Abdo Publishing
abdobooks.com

abdobooks.com

Published by Abdo Publishing, a division of ABDO, PO Box 398166, Minneapolis, Minnesota 55439. Copyright © 2020 by Abdo Consulting Group, Inc. International copyrights reserved in all countries. No part of this book may be reproduced in any form without written permission from the publisher. Super SandCastle™ is a trademark and logo of Abdo Publishing.

Printed in the United States of America, North Mankato, Minnesota
052019
092019

THIS BOOK CONTAINS RECYCLED MATERIALS

Design: Tamara JM Peterson, Mighty Media, Inc.
Production: Mighty Media, Inc.
Editor: Megan Borgert-Spaniol
Cover Photographs: Mighty Media, Inc.; Shutterstock Images
Interior Photographs: iStockphoto; Mighty Media, Inc.; Shutterstock Images; Wikimedia Commons

The following manufacturers/names appearing in this book are trademarks:
Adhesive Tech™, Commercial Electric™, Swingline®

Library of Congress Control Number: 2018967159

Publisher's Cataloging-in-Publication Data

Names: Olson, Elsie, author.
Title: Design survival clothing your way!: crafting weatherproof wearables / by Elsie Olson
Other title: Crafting weatherproof wearables
Description: Minneapolis, Minnesota : Abdo Publishing, 2020 | Series: Super simple diy survival
Identifiers: ISBN 9781532119743 (lib. bdg.) | ISBN 9781532174506 (ebook)
Subjects: LCSH: Outdoor recreation--Safety measures--Juvenile literature. | Survival skills--Juvenile literature. | Camping--Equipment and supplies--Juvenile literature. | Do-it-yourself work--Juvenile literature.
Classification: DDC 613.69--dc23

Super SandCastle™ books are created by a team of professional educators, reading specialists, and content developers around five essential components—phonemic awareness, phonics, vocabulary, text comprehension, and fluency—to assist young readers as they develop reading skills and strategies and increase their general knowledge. All books are written, reviewed, and leveled for guided reading and early reading intervention programs for use in shared, guided, and independent reading and writing activities to support a balanced approach to literacy instruction.

TO ADULT HELPERS

The projects in this book are fun and simple. There are just a few things to remember to keep kids safe. Some projects may use sharp or hot objects. Also, kids may be using messy supplies. Make sure they protect their clothes and work surfaces. Be ready to offer guidance during brainstorming and assist when necessary.

CONTENTS

BECOME A MAKER

A makerspace is like a laboratory. It's a place where ideas are formed and problems are solved. Kids like you create wonderful things in makerspaces. Many makerspaces are in schools and libraries. But they can also be in kitchens, bedrooms, and backyards. Anywhere can be a makerspace when you use imagination, inspiration, **collaboration**, and problem-solving!

IMAGINATION

This takes you to new places and lets you experience new things. Anything is possible with imagination!

INSPIRATION

This is the spark that gives you an idea. Inspiration can come from almost anywhere!

Makerspace Toolbox

COLLABORATION

Makers work together. They ask questions and get ideas from everyone around them. **Collaboration** solves problems that seem impossible.

PROBLEM-SOLVING

Things often don't go as planned when you're creating. But that's part of the fun! Find creative **solutions** to any problem that comes up. These will make your project even better.

SKILLS TO SURVIVE

Being a maker means being ready for anything. Your makerspace toolbox can even help you survive! People with survival skills learn to think fast and problem-solve. They find ways to stay safe and get help in **dangerous** situations.

You don't have to be in danger to use survival skills. These skills can come in handy when you're getting ready to go for a hike or play outside. You can use your survival skills to **design** the perfect **weatherproof** clothing!

PROBLEM-SOLVE!
See page 26

BASIC NEEDS

Imagine you are lost in the woods or caught in a storm. What do you do? To survive, humans must make sure their basic needs are met. When you're building gear to help you survive, keep these basic needs in mind!

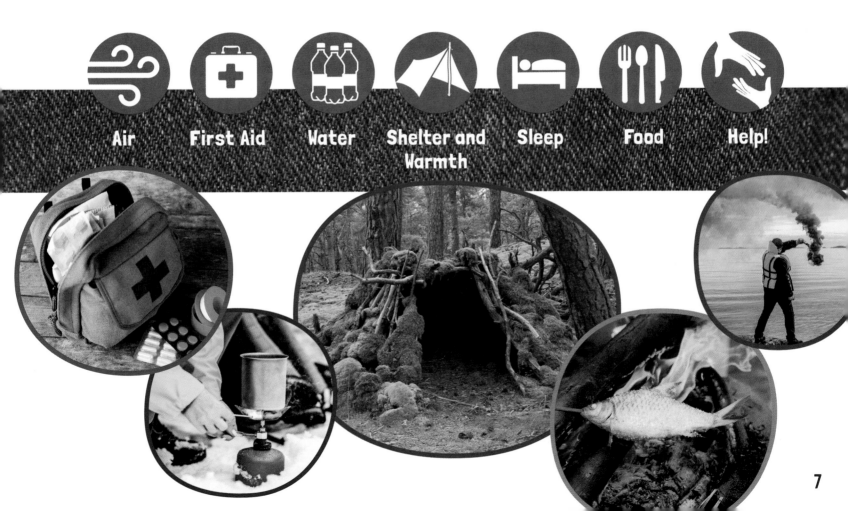

Air   **First Aid**   **Water**   **Shelter and Warmth**   **Sleep**   **Food**   **Help!**

IMAGINE SURVIVAL CLOTHING

DISCOVER AND EXPLORE

Think about the things you wear every day. You might wear a favorite T-shirt to school. Or sneakers to gym class. But wearables can also keep you warm, dry, or otherwise protected from the elements. And with a little creativity, they can do much more!

GET INSPIRED!
See page 24

IMAGINE

If you could **design** your own **weatherproof** clothing, what would it do? Would it keep you cool in the heat? Would it shield you against wind? Then, imagine a situation where you could use the clothing to survive. Are you lost in the Sahara Desert? Are you exploring the North Pole? Remember, there are no rules. Let your imagination run wild!

9

DESIGN SURVIVAL CLOTHING

It's time to turn your dream clothing into a makerspace marvel! Think about your imaginary wearables and survival situation. How can the features of your clothing help you survive? How could you use the materials around you to create these features? Where would you begin?

INSPIRATION

Survival suits are special full-body suits. They are **designed** to keep the wearer warm and dry if she falls into cold water. The suits help the wearer float. They are also brightly colored so they are easy to spot.

COLLABORATE!
See page 28

BE SAFE, BE RESPECTFUL
MAKERSPACE ETIQUETTE

THERE ARE JUST A FEW RULES TO FOLLOW WHEN YOU ARE CRAFTING YOUR SURVIVAL CLOTHING:

1. **ASK FOR PERMISSION AND ASK FOR HELP.** Make sure an adult says it's OK to make your wearables. Get help when using sharp tools, such as a craft knife, or hot tools, like a glue gun.

2. **BE NICE.** Share supplies and space with other makers.

3. **THINK IT THROUGH.** Don't give up when things don't work out exactly right. Instead, think about the problem you are having. What are some ways to solve it?

4. **CLEAN UP.** Put materials away when you are finished working. Find a safe space to store unfinished projects until next time.

WHAT WILL YOUR WEARABLES DO?

How will your clothing help you meet your basic needs? Knowing this will help you figure out which materials to use.

Will it help keep you dry? Then be sure to use **waterproof** materials.

PROBLEM-SOLVE!
See page 26

Will it keep the hot sun off your face?
Then it needs to cast a large shadow. Maybe it's reflective!

Any hat should fit snuggly around your head. Use a flexible material, such as craft foam, to create a comfortable fit.

IMAGINE

WHAT IF YOUR UMBRELLA HAT NEEDED TO PROTECT YOU FROM HAIL? HOW WOULD THAT CHANGE THE MATERIALS YOU USE?

13

Roald Amundsen was a Norwegian explorer. He was the first person to visit the South Pole! Amundsen traveled with 52 sled dogs. He stored food and supplies along the way. That way he could use them during his return trip. Amundsen reached the South Pole in December 1911.

Eyelashes protect our eyes from sand and dust. What materials could serve the same function?

Will it be used in a desert sandstorm? Then you'll need to fully cover your eyes!

14

COLLABORATE!
See page 28

Will it keep you warm? Then use **insulating** materials.

⚠ STUCK?

YOU CAN ALWAYS CHANGE YOUR MIND IN A MAKERSPACE. IS YOUR VEST NOT QUITE WARM ENOUGH? ADD SLEEVES AND MAKE IT A COAT!

15

CRAFT YOUR CLOTHING

Clothing wraps around the shapes and angles of your body. That means it must be lightweight, comfortable, and somewhat **flexible**. Look around for materials that could fit your form!

SEARCH YOUR SPACE

The perfect shape might be in your kitchen cabinet, garage, or toy chest. Search for materials that might seem surprising!

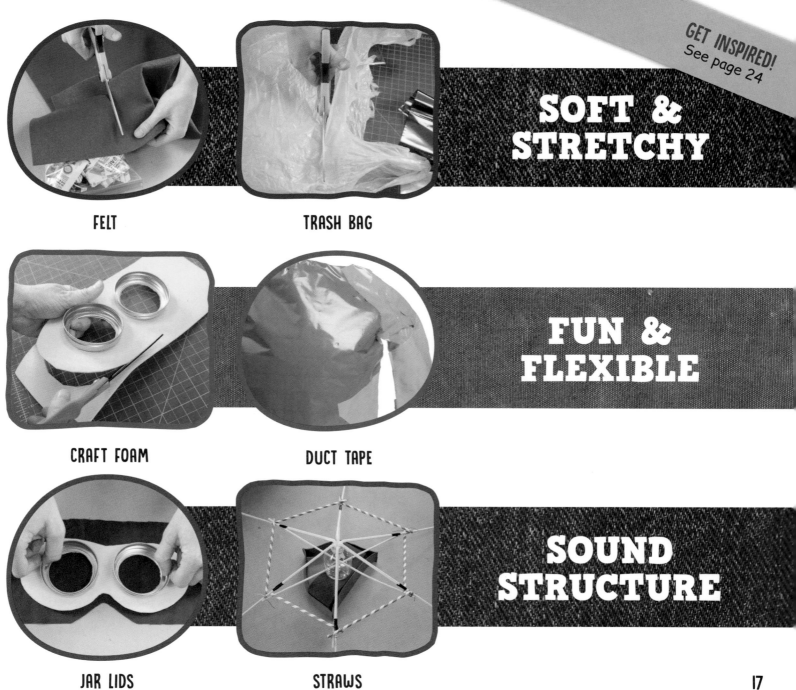

GET INSPIRED!
See page 24

SOFT & STRETCHY

FELT

TRASH BAG

FUN & FLEXIBLE

CRAFT FOAM

DUCT TAPE

SOUND STRUCTURE

JAR LIDS

STRAWS

CONNECT YOUR CLOTHING

Will your clothing be **permanent**? Or will you take it apart when you are finished? Knowing this will help you decide what materials to use.

TOTALLY TEMPORARY

STRING

CHENILLE STEMS

RUBBER BANDS

COLLABORATE!
See page 28

IMAGINE

WHAT IF YOUR RAINSUIT
WERE MADE FOR VISITING
ICY PLUTO? HOW WOULD
THAT CHANGE ITS DESIGN?

A LITTLE STICKY

SUPER STICKY

STAPLES

ELECTRICAL TAPE

HOT GLUE

DUCT TAPE

DECORATE YOUR CLOTHING

Decorating is the final step in making your survival clothing. It's where you add **details** to your wearables. How do these decorations help your clothing do its job?

FELT

CELLOPHANE

CHENILLE STEMS

IMAGINE

WHAT IF YOU WERE CREATING PROTECTIVE GOGGLES FOR AN EIGHT-EYED SPIDER? HOW WOULD THAT CHANGE HOW THEY LOOK?

GET INSPIRED!
See page 24

COOL COLOR

STAY SNUG

FELT

CELLOPHANE

PLASTIC BAG ZIPPER

TRASH BAG DRAWSTRING

DUCT TAPE

HELPFUL HACKS

As you work, you might discover ways to make challenging tasks easier. Try these simple tricks and **techniques** as you build your **weatherproof** wearables!

Create a cardboard pattern for cutting out uniform shapes.

Use straws, skewers, and a plastic bottle to create a lightweight structure.

Stuff plastic bags into the clothing to give it shape and support while you decorate it.

PROBLEM-SOLVE!
See page 26

Test out which materials are **waterproof** before you start crafting.

Cut circles out of a clear plastic bag to make goggle lenses.

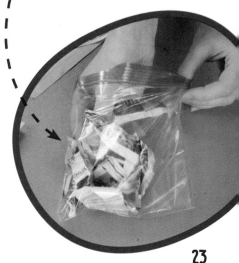

Stuff plastic bags with newspaper for **insulation**.

⚠ STUCK?

MAKERS AROUND THE WORLD SHARE THEIR PROJECTS ON THE INTERNET AND IN BOOKS. IF YOU HAVE A MAKERSPACE PROBLEM, THERE'S A GOOD CHANCE SOMEONE ELSE HAS ALREADY FOUND A SOLUTION. SEARCH THE INTERNET OR LIBRARY FOR HELPFUL ADVICE AS YOU MAKE YOUR PROJECTS!

23

GET INSPIRED

Get inspiration from the real world before you start crafting your wearables!

LOOK AT OUTDOOR CLOTHING

Look at snowsuits, hats, sunglasses, and boots. What features do you notice? How could you use some of these features in your clothing?

Many animals have features that help them survive. Camels have long eyelashes that keep sand out of their eyes. Arctic seals have **insulating** fat to keep them warm. Beavers have special fur that keeps water off their skin.

LOOK AT WILDLIFE

LOOK AT A MAP

Get inspiration by surprising yourself! Close your eyes and point to any spot on a map. Then learn about the climate and **terrain** of the place you pointed to. Pretend you are planning a trip to this region. **Design** clothing that could help you survive there!

PROBLEM-SOLVE

No makerspace project goes exactly as planned. But with a little creativity, you can find a **solution** to any problem.

FIGURE OUT THE PROBLEM

Maybe your rainsuit doesn't fit quite right. Why do you think that is? Thinking about what may be causing the problem can lead you to a solution!

★

SOLUTION:
IF IT'S TOO TIGHT, CUT A SEAM TO CREATE MORE SPACE. THEN COVER THE SPACE WITH TAPE.

★

SOLUTION:
IF IT'S TOO LOOSE, CUT A SEAM AND OVERLAP THE MATERIAL. SECURE WITH TAPE.

BRAINSTORM AND TEST

Try coming up with three possible **solutions** to any problem.
Maybe your umbrella hat keeps falling off.
You could:

1. Make sure the weight of the structure is balanced.

2. Use a different material for the headband.

3. Add a chin strap to hold it on your head.

ADAPT

Still stuck? Try a different material
or change the **technique** slightly.

COLLABORATE

Collaboration means working together with others. There are tons of ways to collaborate to create **weatherproof** wearables!

ASK A FELLOW MAKER

Don't be shy about asking a friend or classmate for help on your project. Other makers can help you think through the different steps to crafting survival clothing. These helpers can also lend a hand during construction!

ASK AN ADULT HELPER

This could be a parent, teacher, grandparent, or any trusted adult. Tell this person about the most important function or feature of your clothing. Your grown-up helper might think of materials or **techniques** you never would have thought of!

ASK AN EXPERT

Talk to people who camp, mountain climb, or do other outdoor activities. Find out what clothing they wear to stay comfortable. Ask fashion **designers** how they turn their ideas into real wearables.

THE WORLD IS A MAKERSPACE!

Your survival clothing may look finished, but don't close your makerspace toolbox yet. Think about what would make your wearables better. What would you do differently if you crafted them again? What would happen if you used different **techniques** or materials?

IMAGINATION

INSPIRATION

COLLABORATION

PROBLEM-SOLVING

DON'T STOP AT CLOTHING

You can use your makerspace toolbox beyond the makerspace! You might use it to accomplish everyday tasks, such as making a homemade gift or inventing a new game. But makers use the same toolbox to do big things. One day, these tools could help build rockets or save animals from **extinction**. Turn your world into a makerspace! What problems could you solve?

GLOSSARY

collaborate – to work with others.

dangerous – able or likely to cause harm or injury.

design – to plan how something will appear or work. A design is a sketch or outline of something that will be made. A designer is someone who plans how something will appear or work.

detail – a small part of something.

extinction – the state of no longer existing.

flexible – easy to move or bend.

insulate – to keep heat or cold in or out. Insulation is a material that keeps heat or cold in or out.

permanent – meant to last for a very long time.

solution – an answer to, or a way to solve, a problem.

technique – a method or style in which something is done.

terrain – an area of land or the physical features of an area of land.

waterproof – made so that water can't get in.

weatherproof – able to withstand or protect against sun, rain, or other weather conditions.